I0711214

Preface

This book is a sampling of the ideas of liberty. If the arguments in this book leave you compelled to dive into it more then be sure to check out these websites with free articles and books, curriculums and podcasts.

Websites

Tom Woods- one of most well known modern-day Libertarians

Ludwig Von Mises Institute

Foundations of Economics Education

Anti War

Curriculum

Liberty Classroom (Liberty from POV of Libertarianism)

Ron Paul's self-taught homeschooling curriculum

Podcasts

The Tom Woods Show

The Libertarian Christian Podcast

The Anarcho Christian Podcast

The Bob Murphy Show

Radio Rothbard

Ron Paul Liberty Podcast

Table of Contents

Part 2: Privatized over Public

Part 3: Compatibility of Conservative Christianity and Libertarianism

Introduction to Libertarian

"I'm a libertarian in part because I see a false choice offered by the political left and right: government control of the economy—or government control of our personal lives. People on both sides think of themselves as freedom lovers. The left thinks the government can lessen income inequality. The right thinks the government can make Americans more virtuous. I say we're best off if neither side attempts to advance its agenda via government." [1]

Most of my adult life I hated politics. I never could fully agree with either side of the spectrum. I thought the left wanted to have too big of government and the right was too abusive of the left. I liked the pro-capitalism of the right but hated the socialism of the left. In libertarianism, I saw a governmental theory that allows for all people to coexist and does not give the government the potential for unlimited moral or economic power.

---

[1] Tom Palmer, Why Liberty: Your Life, Your Choices, Your Future, 2.

I write this book not as a political science major but as a citizen in pursuit of clarity. I aim explore libertarianism as the reasonable and much needed alternative to our common political understanding.

I am a rideshare driver (at the time of writing this book) and many times when I get into a conversation about politics with a millennial (the generation which is the up and coming workforce), they say they want all of us to meet in the middle. The problem with that is each individual has a worldview and convictions that come from that worldview. Whether they say there is absolute truth or not doesn't really matter in reality. Everyone has opinions about most things. So to tell someone that they should abandon their stance for the sake of "getting along" is not a reasonable desire. People's convictions are forged by the sacred text, the experience they have had in life, and the teaching they have received from others. They are not just willing to give up their inner compass to the map of life for the sake of bowing to this forced middle way.

So, for those of you who are tired of the divide and the infighting continue reading to hear of an option that can be a great potential option to actually bring us together without moral compromise on the part of the individual. Then join me on the journey to discover the value of Liberty over all other potential benefits.

Side note: I want to be clear, most of the quotes in the first part of the book are from Tom Palmer because I wanted to keep the book simple and not overrun with a bunch of quotes from a bunch of different people. I just wanted to give a simple explanation and stream line that.

Chapter 1: Two principles of Libertarianism

Libertarianism at its core can be defined by two major principles. Libertarianism only allows for legislation to be passed that protects the citizen's property and body of any country. What I mean by protecting is that those who actually are tasked with serving mankind are those that their job description falls in line with one of these two things. This would mainly include policemen, firemen, and paramedics. (Some libertarians argue that these jobs could be privatized) Consider that Doctors are paid privately through insurance companies that are mainly funded by the free market. They provide a service to protect people's bodies from harm but they are paid privately. People are willing to pay for the things they see as necessary. Most Libertarians agree that the rest of society will be privatized, outside of those two jobs that serve protection. This includes courtroom jobs, sewage department, parks and recreation department, libraries, public schools, etc. I know what the average person thinks, how will society function if those things go private? Well, the things that people see as necessary, they will be willing to pay for. People are already paying for these services through taxation, so the government would not tax them for these things and they would use said money for these services.

The misunderstanding about these services is that people think they are free because they are not charged a recurring payment for the services in order to gain membership or continue to use the services. However, they are paying for them, and against their will at that.

What I mean by against their will is that the government requires people in society to pay for libraries through taxation even if they don't want the libraries or use them. If people do not pay the government taxes, they are treated like criminals and will be forced to pay for what the government deems necessary.

If libertarianism reigned in America then people would vote for the library by purchasing a membership or not. The libraries now function no matter how slow they get. They do not function as a normal business, they are kept afloat by tax funds, and these government organizations should be subject to the free market. In a subscription-based business, they will be purged of bad ideas or outdated ideas. If perceived us unworthy of continuing they will be put out of business and replaced. The winner is the patron who gets the best quality experience.

Chapter 2: The Historical Significance of Liberty

"Libertarianism (the contemporary name for principled classical liberalism) has already profoundly shaped the modern world. In much of the world, many battles have already been fought and in many places won: separation of church and state; limitation of power through constitutions: freedom of speech; debunking mercantilism and replacing it with free trade; abolition of slavery;

personal freedom and legal toleration for minorities, whether religious, ethnic, linguistic, or sexual; protection of property; the defeat of Fascism, Jim Crow, Apartheid, and Communism. Far too many intellectuals and activists to name made those victories possible, but they made the world better—more just, more peaceful, and freer. They made the libertarian position on those and many other issues the baseline for reasonable political discourse." [2]

---

[2] Tom Palmer, Why Liberty: Your Life, Your Choices, Your Future, 25.

When people think of conservatives who believe in small or limited government, they think that we are just government haters and we want to be able to have freedom so that we can attack oppress others, but it is not the case. Those who want to limit the government do so because they value the freedom of the individual. We have a healthy fear of the government's potential to oppress and limit the people. In our minds, if the governments are limited then the people can be unlimited in their potential. If the government is big than the government is potentially unlimited and naturally will limit the individuals because they will pass more laws.

Libertarianism has always been a political principle that believes all individual worldviews and belief systems should be able to exist in the world we live in. Tom Palmer describes it like this, "Libertarian ideas about rights were forged largely in the struggle for religious freedom and for the freedom of the weak who suffered oppression from the strong." [3] Those of us who are religious, or those of us who are less fortunate, should not be treated as "less thens" or "outcasts". Libertarianism is all about protecting what we believe in against any outside powers, or people

---

[3] Tom Palmer, Why Liberty: Your Life, Your Choices, Your Future, 38.

that might want to take it away due to disagreement.

Historically civilizations have always been run by either one individual or small groups of individuals functioning like one mind. Whether it was the Emperors of the Roman and Greek empires, the Pharaohs of Egypt or the kings over the ages, they all wanted to control the people. Their mentality was always the control of people because that is what's best for them. They do not believe that freedom could bring about a better society they were afraid of fear or freedom so instead, they told the people that they should believe in submission and subservience. This is why most rulers had one established religion for all the people on their land. If somebody had a different religious belief, it was very hard for them to exist in society due to persecution. Most people would have to flee or migrate to another society that had the same beliefs as them.

From Faith to Freedom

America was founded on the hope of religious freedom initially. The Church of England was the one main religion of England that had been established by Queen Elizabeth.

She saw the fighting between Protestants and Catholics and decides to merge the two religions into one. Which we now know it as the Church of England or the Anglican Church. This outraged the Protestants. Combining two different religions was not cohesive and consistent with their beliefs. They unwillingly endured their clear definitive teaching on each doctrine of the church being watered down for the sake of political influence.

The first settlers of America took the libertarian ideal to heart, came to America and became The Separatist. The Separatists wanted to come to America because they could not stand being denied the freedom of practicing their own religion. Initially, many agreed with the Separatist but preferred to demonstrate their patriotism by fixing the country they loved instead of fleeing to uncharted lands. Some Protestants that didn't agree with the Church of England, but thought that they were called by God to fix it, stayed. These Protestant believers were called the semi-separatists. After many frustrating years, they realized the church was too established and too set in their ways to consider alternatives. So they decided to follow the separatist to America so they could function with their own religion without being oppressed or persecuted by the established church of England.

Without libertarianism, America would've taken much longer to be colonized. The desire to be free and have our individual rights protected was so strong in those few thousand people that they were willing to cross the sea risking death, and start over with nothing more than whatever they happened to be carrying. This was the first time that a country was founded purely on the desire for freedom of religion. Historically new countries, wars, and charting of new lands were meant for furthering a country's agenda. For example, Spain wanted to spread its Catholicism to the rest of the world, so Cortez crossed the sea trying to find another way to get to Asia so they could share their beliefs with them. Normally the leadership or government would send individuals with the funding of the government to go explore on their behalf, The Separatist were so desperate to get away they were willing to forego any form of government funding and support.

The strong desire to get away from oppression and a one-track mind of thinking will drive many to do unthinkable things under normal circumstances. The Separatists had jobs, families, friends, and property. They left all that they knew to start a whole new society just because they believed in freedom. Libertarians look at this strong desire to live out this principle of freedom as admirable and desirable. Our heart's true conviction is to not be subjugated to government control.

America and its freedom have changed so much of the world, which is why everyone wants to come here, because of that freedom. Why would we willingly give up our freedom in order to have some sort of 'free' amenities? Freedom is something that is priceless, it's more valuable than billions of dollars. Without freedom, all of your happiness can be stripped from you. All of your ability to live by your convictions can be taken from you by the government at its whim if given enough power to do so.

We have made so much progress to get to this new idea of freedom, why would we turn around and give up? Why would we, like the Israelites of the Bible willingly go back to slavery after being freed? Even though it's hard trying to use democracy to establish something less structured, it's worth it.

Tom Palmer describes the newness of libertarian thought like this,

> "Libertarianism as a political philosophy appeared with the modern age. It is the modern philosophy of individual freedom, rather than serfdom or subservience; of legal systems based on the enjoyment of rights, rather than the

exercise of arbitrary power; of mutual prosperity through free labor, voluntary cooperation, and exchange, rather than forced labor, compulsion, and the exploitation of the plundered by their conquerors; and of toleration and mutual co-existence of religions, lifestyles, ethnic groups, and other forms of human existence, rather than religious, tribal, or ethnic warfare. It is the philosophy of the modern world and it is rapidly spreading among young people around the globe." [4]

---

[4] Tom Palmer, Why Liberty: Your Life, Your Choices, Your Future, 29.

The Truth about Slavery

Slavery has always existed. Historically countries tend to make slaves of their conquered opponents. One of the first places to end enslavement was America. The principle behind the rights of slaves to freedom was the libertarian principle of the Declaration of Independence, namely that all men are created equal. Tom Palmer describes how revolutionary these ideas of liberty were in the early centuries of America.

"After the articulation and promotion of the ideas of individual rights, limited government, and political economy during the Enlightenment, the evolving moral consciousness embedded in those ideas could no longer coexist peacefully with the coercion, lawlessness, and violent control imposed on slaves. That was especially true after the adoption of the Declaration of Independence and its insistence that 'all men are created equal.' Inspired by their newfound moral awareness, the early libertarians, including the leaders of the abolitionist movements, worked to shape a world in which the institutions of law, politics, and culture would be in harmony with liberty." [5]

Even though libertarianism as a political group is comprised of fewer constituents than other political parties, the principle behind libertarianism has existed since the founding of America. If anything, <u>libertarianism is the foundational principle that America was built on.</u>

This short historical recap shows you the power of liberty for past generations. The gravity of change that Liberty has had on society historically affects people from all backgrounds, whether rich or poor. Without

---

[5] Tom Palmer, Why Liberty: Your Life, Your Choices, Your Future, 47.

libertarianism we would not have women voting, we would not have African-Americans free from slavery, other freedoms that we have fought for as a country over the decades and centuries. Without libertarianism, we are left with a caste system where the rich are better than the poor, or certain skin tones are better than other skin tones. One should think twice before considering Libertarianism to be illegitimate. The reminder should always be that liberty is the core of Libertarianism, and is foundational to what makes America great. I am going to end this chapter with a quote from Tom Palmer.

"Libertarians blazed the trail by pointing out the harmful effects of prohibition—on morality, on justice, on crime rates, on families, on social order—more and more political leaders are speaking out about the disastrous consequences of the war on drugs without fear of being smeared as "pro-drugs." They include presidents of Mexico, Guatemala, Colombia, and Brazil, countries that have suffered from the crime, the violence, and corruption brought by prohibition, as well as governors, former secretaries of state, judges, police chiefs, and many others."

Chapter 3: Toleration

"The origin of morality is the self: how people ought to act because they, themselves are human beings. The origin of political philosophy is others: the requirement to treat others justly because other people are human beings." [6]

---

[6] Tom Palmer, Why Liberty: Your Life, Your Choices, Your Future, 61.

Libertarianism is summed up as follows "you live your life and exercise your own freedom with respect for the freedom and rights of others. You behave as a libertarian." [7]Libertarianism is respect for people's ability to do what they would like to do. The notion of certain beliefs, thoughts, and actions as immoral and should be regulated by the government is not a libertarian thought. Libertarianism is not the lack of conviction, but a belief that each person should be able to act on a conviction. The right of the individual is the only real right. Political parties or large groups shouldn't be able to get their views in

---

[7] Tom Palmer, Why Liberty: Your Life, Your Choices, Your Future, 10.

government and pressed on all of the individuals of society. The reminder should always be in the hand that liberty is at the core of Libertarianism, and is foundational to what makes America great as long as it does not violate the body or property of another. No regard is necessary for those who feel 'offended'.

Normally the organization that is most able to violate the sanctity of personal conviction, is the government because the government has no higher governing power over itself. The government is the one business with no oversight other than its own inner checks and balances of the three branches:

legislative, executive, and judicial. The problem with this is that it is susceptible to manipulation. Either the branch is too big, leading to bureaucratic stagnation; or the branch is too small, which creates a variable of instability

Chapter 4: Utopia

One thing that I do not understand is why some people think that taking away the rights of other people will bring about the ideal peace everyone imagines in their heads. Utopia does not exist if people lose their freedom that is a dystopia. Tom Palmer describes what true utopia is, "one has the right to do whatever one chooses with what is one's own —to freely follow one's own will, rather than the commands of another, so long as one respects the equal rights of others." [8]

When I used to be an atheist I was fed the idea that if we all believed the same thing it would lead to peace, but now that I actually have conviction, I know that I would not give that up for anything. Some people have very loose convictions that are based on their own

---

[8] Tom Palmer, Why Liberty: Your Life, Your Choices, Your Future, 16.

preferences while many other people who are religious have convictions that are formed by some sort of scripture. Those with convictions founded upon scripture are not going to just forfeit them. The lack of peace in this world is actually people being non-libertarian in their thinking because if you were libertarian you would accept that other people have convictions and beliefs that are different from your own. You would be able to get along with them without being intolerant and aggressive towards their worldview and preferences.

Chapter 5: Dividing line

Tom Palmer summarizes the dividing line between libertarianism and other political theories well when he says "It is the notion of authority that forms the true locus of the dispute between libertarianism and other political philosophies." [9] The libertarian mindset of the government is there to protect liberties, not to take them away. The government is allowed to favor one conviction or liberty to the neglect and the obstruction of other liberties of other individuals. This is why most legislation is illegitimate in a libertarian society. Which

---

[9] Tom Palmer, Why Liberty: Your Life, Your Choices, Your Future, 16.

explains why libertarians are limited government. Most legislation violates the rights of others whether on the conservative side of the spectrum or the liberal side of the spectrum. When legislation is passed in favor of one party over the others, then the other parties will be offended.

One might object that the government's sole purpose is to pass legislation that governs morality, but to govern morality doesn't mean to favor one particular conviction over others. To govern morality ought to mean protecting people's belongings, namely their body and their property. The only morality of the government in a libertarian society does not harm other people by taking from them, neither their wealth nor their health. People can take other people's wealth by stealing from them and people can take someone's health by harming them. So in this sense, the government is regulating morality. Anything more than this is excessive and subjective.

Chapter 6: Democracy

We live in a democracy where people have rights as individuals to not be violated.

Democracy should not be used to pass one particular moral value to the attack or to the oppression of others.

"Some people attempt to legislate morality because they believe that if something is immoral, it obviously ought to be illegal. If people ought not to do it, then others should prevent them from doing it. A common response to this is to say that 'people have different moralities' and they ought not to impose 'their morality' on others. In a totalitarian society, it makes sense to have a government regulate morality because the government by definition is a dictatorship that dictates what's right or wrong, but in a democracy and a representative republic where

the people are free, it does not make any sense

for the government to come in and regulate

people's morality." [10]

Chapter 7: The Recess

Analogy

When I was an after school daycare

helper (when I was in high school), we used to

take the kids to the playground every day to

---

[10] Tom Palmer, Why Liberty: Your Life, Your Choices, Your Future, 61.

play, this experience is the experience where this analogy was drawn from.

When children are in elementary school, the children are young and immature, so the adults set up general rules to keep them from playing unfair and harming one another. In the main area of the playground, where the slides and swings are, the children are playing games like tag. These are games that kids either made up or are playing on an imaginative level. Children play and run around based on simple rules and competitive nature.

Unless the children get upset and lose control, the children play happily with one another. The adults are merely there to

supervise and mediate between the children,
and only intervene when it is necessary.
Otherwise, the children have their own system
of play that develops between them. Each day
they come out to play on the playground and as
young humans grow and mature together. The
strong win in a context where strength is best
suited and the smart children win where smarts
are most needed. Children who lack strength
and intelligence struggle to win amidst their
weakness.

This analogy shows a functioning
libertarian society. The teachers do not tell the
children the rules of their games. They are not
dictating which games are economically or

morally incorrect. They are not trying to enforce any manufactured equalizer. The children are regulating themselves by creating their own rules for the games and co-playing in the little society that they have created for themselves. This ecosystem is daily, although it is for a short period of time, it is steady and consistently held meeting time so that they can establish their own norms. This ecosystem is able to thrive because schools implement "the free society principle", Tom Palmer describes this rule like this, "the rules of free societies are not crafted to benefit this or that person or group; they respect the rights of every human being, regardless of gender, color, religion, language, family, or other accidental feature."[11]

Which explains why children of all shapes and sizes, skin tones, and abilities are able to coexist and play along with each other even with their advantages and disadvantages. The children except one another how they are and are able to get along because of their toleration and acceptance of one another's scenario that they find themselves in, physically and emotionally.

You might argue that this analogy is using too simple of an example. I would argue that you are correct, that children do not have a currency based system or strong moral convictions having to be acted out in their

---

[11] Tom Palmer, Why Liberty: Your Life, Your Choices, Your Future, 17.

childish games, but what they do have is tolerance. The children desire to get along because they are one another's means of social interaction, competition, and entertainment.

Most of the country has people in public areas interacting with each other in an agreeable manner. We see someone who is Muslim praying towards Mecca or a homosexual couple holding hands and most people accept that it is their belief and life choice, even if they personally don't agree. Why do we need the government to pass legislation that condemns certain people that hold different views?

I was an Atheist until the age of 16. As a Christian, I do not wish for the government to pass legislation discriminating against Atheists. If I had not come to believe in the Christian message by God's grace, I would surely still be an Atheist today. We all must come to realize that we are shaped by our experiences. One person might have grown up in a Buddhist family, and so naturally, they are going to be inclined to Buddhism until otherwise convinced.

It seems contradictory to raise children to tolerate other children's beliefs, but then when they become adults to allow them to pass legislation that's going to attack the same beliefs that they were told to tolerate. Schools, in general, are built on the libertarian mindset of freedom of beliefs, you have all kinds of different children in schools with different believes but the administration doesn't come to those students and tell them that they have to believe X thing that they have established as the general morality for that school. (Private schools are the exception, but the school is built on the idea of exclusivity so that parents can have their children in an environment that affirms their beliefs instead of contradicting them) The only exception would be the two principles that libertarianism believes are core, don't hit other kids and don't steal their property. Why have we complicated things once we become adults, why can we not keep it

as simple as elementary school rules?

Chapter 8: Freedom with Free Market

Economically, libertarians put their hope

in the free market instead of the government.

We believe that the government should leave

people to do what they will and in the midst of

the freedom of spontaneous choice there will

come a prosperous society. Quality employees

get paid well for their skills because they add value to the company. The free market allows people to put themselves out there for other companies to snatch them up for more adequate pay.

So if somebody wants to be able to make more money than they can learn skills and get more experience in any given field or industry and that will make them more valuable. Yes, upfront they might have to use money but they could do loans and get scholarships. Since they will make more money they can pay that off. How do you think doctors and lawyers logically justify the amount they spend on school? They know they will make it back ten-fold. In the

short term they lose money, but they outpace it
in the long term.

Chapter 9: Free Market and Big American Companies

Tom Palmer hits the nail on the head when he says, "Being a libertarian means understanding how wealth is created; not by politicians giving commands, but by free people working together, inventing, creating, saving, investing, buying and selling, all based on respect for the property, that is, the rights, of others" [12] The biggest companies in the world like Amazon, Apple, Google, Facebook were built on people making free choices of wanting to build wealth via having a new idea that's helpful to people. Facebook was built on the idea of allowing people to really concentrate the ability for people on the Internet to live in community and communicate really efficiently with one another, even more efficiently than forms and email because those already exist. Apple wanted to create devices that allow people to efficiently use apps and the Internet (phone calls and texts were already being down

---

[12] Tom Palmer, Why Liberty: Your Life, Your Choices, Your Future, 16.

well before Apple.) Google wanted to help people find the answers to their questions, find a person or a company they were looking for. Amazon was trying to help people be able to find a product that they wanted without having to go get into the car and drive to the store or the mall. People can just go online and have an interface that put X product in front of them that was relevant to them that they already wanted to buy. If the government were to have had extreme regulations and limitations on the free market back when all these companies were created then they probably would not exist.

Through innovation, we have been allowed to come into the modern age of technology. People want to be able to have a society with socialism (taxpayer-funded stuff) but they don't want to give up all the benefits of having a free market (technological and industrial advances). Without a free market, America wouldn't be the strongest country in the nation and we wouldn't have all the benefits that we have. I understand the desire to not want there to be poor people but, as I said earlier, anyone can become educated and learn skills and make themselves more valuable. There are so many different ways you can make money these days because of the free market. To where you don't need to have a boss or get

hired or interview for a job you can just have
the minimum requirements for it and then just
go directly to the client through a middleman
app like Uber. These apps are allowing people
to not have to be poor even if they have little
skill. For example with Uber, all you need is a
car with four doors and a driver's license, and
you can make as much money as you want to. I
provide for my family with my sole income
from Uber. At the time of writing this book
(Not advocating for welfare system just making
a point on how much money an app is provided
for my own family)

Chapter 10: Free Market and Limitless Income Potential

The free market has allowed for these income sources that take a little or very little skills and experience to be able to make a side income to help increase your total revenue on a daily or weekly basis. So I think it's more of a lack of drive and apathy then it is an opportunity to make money. If you're willing to put in the time and the money you can make potentially unlimited money. People are just so focused on "I'm only making this much an hour" but they don't consider that they could just put in more hours in something else. Because no matter what you're going to put in more time to make money; whether you learning a skill or you going have to do something that's a low skill level (just be able to drive) but have to trade time for money like Uber, Postmates, Favor or some sort of a handyman app whatever it might be. The only way those companies were even able to exist is in a free-market society. The other side is that Uber is limited in certain markets because the government has a deal with the taxis to where they're not allowed to be in the city or be at the airport. (At the time of writing this book)

Which is only hurting the people who want to just make some extra income or want to do it full-time and it's hurting the people who just want to get to the bar or back from the bar, or to the airport or back from the airport, or to the back from the car dealership and back over to the car dealership or whatever might be going on. The regulations are limiting people from getting a service that they are willing to pay for. They should be allowing the free market to destroy any company that is not doing their job well or are overpriced. Instead, they are propping up companies that the people would not normally want if there is a better option.

Chapter 11: Free Market and Spontaneous Decisions

"Free markets incorporate more, not less, order and foresight than coercively directed or commanded societies. The spontaneous order of markets is far more abstract, complex, and farsighted than all the five-year plans or economic interventions ever devised." [13]

---

[13] Tom Palmer, Why Liberty: Your Life, Your Choices, Your Future, 18.

The free market allows for us as the consumer to pull the plug on a company like for example Apple because let's say Apple does something scandalous tomorrow, everyone can pull out of Apple and it would die very quickly. That's the power of the free market as the power of choosing to vote or not vote, for this company with your wallet and giving towards their products or their services. And this thinking allows us to have the best of the best companies. The ones that are not worthy are being left at the bottom to make less profit or they're dying off, but then the people who are experiencing the best companies are happy and satisfied because they're getting the best bang for their buck.

The more that we regulate the free market, the more likely it is that we're going to get low-quality products and services because if the government gains control of it we will have government selected companies that the government will control and fund. Instead, we can use "Institutions which emerge when people are free to exchange, help to guide resources to their most highly valued uses, without vesting coercive power in a bureaucracy." [14] People really desire order and community around the same ideas products and industries. This thirst to gather around the commonality has always existed and always

---

[14] Tom Palmer, Why Liberty: Your Life, Your Choices, Your Future, 18.

happens in the matter of what society or timeline you look at throughout history. There is no need for the business of the government to come in and control which companies should thrive.

I will end this chapter with an analogy. If you were a server at a restaurant and you work your butt off and you earn $300 in tips, would you rather walk out that night with $300 that you earned or would you rather put your money into a general tip pool and then have it evenly divided up where each person walks out with $100 a pop? Is that really fair to you, does that make you want to go work your butt off and make $300 bucks or does that make you want to go and make $50 a night and still get paid $100? Nobody in their right mind wants to put in the energy for $300 and then get $200 of that $300 stolen from them. But socialism is trying to tell you that oh we can't have a person making only 25 bucks a night so you need to lose 2/3 of your income in order to make it to where we all make the same amount of money by the end of the day. But that takes away all incentive to make any money that takes away the desire to be an amazing server or whatever job you might be doing because of their insufficient compensation for what you do.

Chapter 12: Forced Morality

Libertarians don't believe that the government should be the ones to force a particular view on individuals instead individual citizens share with one another from a citizen to citizen level. In that sense libertarianism still keeps democracy where we all are free people doing what we really want to do. The difference between libertarian democracy and bipartisan democracy is libertarianism does not allow people to take their individual moral beliefs system and put it into the government as the one standard above all others, instead, we allow for people to freely live life as they want. In that sense, it is a government by the people and for the people, because it is for all the people not just the majority of them.

Throughout history when one system was put as the standard over all others; it led to persecution, oppression, belittlement, imprisonment, Etc. Tom Palmer describes libertarian's purpose and function in the political spectrum, "Libertarians could be said to occupy the radical center of political discourse. . . One could call us centrist in the sense that from the center we project our ideas

outward and inform political parties and

ideologies across the spectrum." [15]

Chapter 13: Individual

Freedom

Libertarianism is a political philosophy

centered on the importance of individual

liberty. Due to this focus on individual liberty

____

[15] Tom Palmer, Why Liberty: Your Life, Your
Choices, Your Future

"A libertarian can be 'socially conservative' or 'socially progressive,' urban or rural, religious or not, a teetotaler or a drinker, married or single." [16]

I, a conservative Baptist white male, can be a libertarian with a liberal atheist African female. We can coexist and believe in the same principle of freedom. We can have a different moral stance on what individuals should do when it comes to belief, but we can still co-exist under the banner of "Liberty advocates".

An example of this is me. I used to be an atheist. I could have been libertarian then just

---

[16] Tom Palmer, Why Liberty: Your Life, Your Choices, Your Future, 24.

as much as I am now. This is why the principle of Liberty is a centrist political stance. We can all (except for the socialist) come under one roof and say yes and amen to Liberty for all. Even though in our hearts and minds we are thinking of different liberties that should be defended.

Chapter 14: The Elephant in the Room

"Republicans and Libertarians share

ground on some policies. They are,

generally, both in favor of economic

freedom, national defense, respect of

property rights, and the right to bear

arms. Clear issues of departure between

the two groups arise when you begin

discussing social issues, like drug

legalization, abortion, and same-sex

---

[17] Kevin D. Gomez

(http://www.genfkd.org/explaining-

difference-between-libertarians-and-

republicans)

marriage. Republicans will advocate for the prohibition of these actions while Libertarians are in favor of a more 'you do you' stance." [17]

From an economic standpoint, the libertarians and Republicans agree on many things. The main difference is that the Republicans believe in the regulation of drugs because they deem drugs as immoral. In the libertarian mind, we see the Republican desire to regulate morality as inconsistent with the desire for limited government and freedom. The government should be limited both morally and economically. The Republicans in one breath will say we should be allowed to defend

ourselves with guns, and in the next breath say

that the government should be able to keep

somebody from marrying the same sex. It

seems to be a little inconsistent to allow

somebody the freedom of defending themselves

but not the freedom to marry somebody of the

same sex.

Libertarians are through and through

about liberty whether morally or economically.

We don't believe in giving people some

freedoms and then taking away other freedoms.

Just because we as individual citizens disagree

with something morally does not mean that we

think that the government shouldn't force or

limit people from being able to do it. Will

making same-sex marriage an illegal bring

down the number of same-sex relationships, no

not all? Will making drugs illegal stop anybody

from partaking in drugs, not at all? The

Republicans buy into the idea that if we

regulate it from the government then the

individual citizens will bow down and follow

suit.   The Republicans are sending mixed

messages to people. They're saying you should

be able to defend yourself from a tyrannical

government but you should submit to the

government when it says you are not allowed to

have drugs.

I speak to you Republicans in this way because I want to plead to you logically that your view is inconsistent. I myself grew up a Republican, I am a third-generation Republican. My father and my father's father are both conservative Republicans. So when I speak to you I don't speak to you as a former enemy but a friend. I have a lot of respect for the Republican's desire to defend our liberties, but I just think that the Republican Party has not gone far enough.

The Republican Party should not be able to tell the government they can't regulate the economy but then turn around and tell the government that they want them to regulate people's morality. We need to believe in the liberty of all kinds. Republicans have pretended that you can have a middle way, where you can give some liberties but not others, but I believe this is cherry-picking and subjective.

Tom Palmer puts it like this,

> "Why be libertarian? It may sound glib, but a reasonable response is, Why not? Just as the burden of proof is on the one who accuses another of a crime, not on the one accused, the burden of proof is on the one who would deny liberty to another person, not the one who would exercise liberty." [18]

---

[18] Tom Palmer, Why Liberty: Your Life, Your

So I ask you Republicans why are you trying to take away other people's liberties? Why would you give people some liberties and not others? What makes the liberties that the Democrats want less valuable than the liberties that you want? Do you see that it's very subjective to whoever happens to be within power? Don't you think you're contradicting yourself by choosing some freedoms and not others?

This is the very thing I had to grapple with as a young man. I agreed with the Republican Party that we should have economic freedom and then I looked over at the

---

Democratic Party and heard their arguments that their morality should not be regulated by the government. I came to realize it was just a fickle king of the hill back-and-forth between the two parties. The bipartisan set up never allows the two parties to make progress but instead creates enemies out of those who value different liberties.

We all should resonate with this quote,

> "Beyond the small amount needed to fund a highly limited government, let no one forcibly take other people's money. When in doubt, leave it out—or rather, leave it to the market and other voluntary institutions." [19]

So if we can agree that people's money shouldn't be taken from them, then why their X product should be taken away from them or why should the ability to express their love for another is taken away from them? Why are people free to spend their money on which hamburger they want to get but they're not free to partake in whatever drug they want? Why can people go to a doctor and buy the individual pieces of hard drugs that make the drugs but once they put them together they become illegal? It's very logically inconsistent to have such arbitrary laws like these.

---

[19] Tom Palmer, Why Liberty: Your Life, Your Choices, Your Future, 20.

America was originally founded by the freedom of church and state for this very reason. The government is not meant to come and establish one rule of morality over all the others. I can agree with you that I think that people should stay away from hard drugs and that homosexual marriage is immoral and against God's design for marriage, but that's my individual belief as one citizen. I don't think that my individual believes should be put on to the rest of the country. Also just to be clear I have purposefully not dealt with the third part of the earlier quoted abortion because I will deal with that more fully in a later chapter specifically devoted to abortion being murder and thus inconsistent with libertarianism.

Chapter 15: Millennials and Socialism

Check out this Gallop poll on millennials, "57% of Democrats hold a favorable view toward socialism, while a record low for the same party now say they support capitalism." [20]

My generation, the millennials, are drinking the Kool-Aid when it comes to socialism. We need to ban together as co-promoters of liberty and propagate the new up-and-coming generation and tell them of the historical woes and failures of socialism and communism. As I said, a chapter back, Republicans need to lay down their moral preference and superiority and come to the middle ground and reach out to the socialist without any sort of moral tension nor moral agitation. I'm not saying that you should stop

---

[20] Investors Business Daily, https://www.investors.com/politics/editorials/millennials-socialism/

believing what you believe I am just saying that

in order to help all kinds of people from getting

stuck in the lies of socialism we need to be

more open to people that we disagree with.

We need to buy into, what we discussed

in the earlier chapter of, peer to peer influence.

Just passing a law is not going to change

people's behavior. The only chance that we

have for saving the millennials from buying

into socialism ensuring this country, America,

is to put down all of our biases and to speak the

truth of the limitations and failures of socialism

in a country.

We must warn millennials of the past

tyrannies like, "Venezuela, Cuba, Nicaragua,

Zimbabwe and North Korea, (because these)

ideas have never delivered equality, better lives,

more opportunity, a sense of belonging,

freedom or anything else that young people say

they want."

(https://www.investors.com/politics/editorials/

millennials-socialism)

These young people want ideals, but the

government can never give ideals. The

government can only take away freedoms it

cannot give freedoms. The bigger the

government gets, the fewer freedoms there are

left over for people to have, and such is the

nature of more power is less freedom.

The writer at investors summarizes the threat well, "What is the greatest threat today to freedom and the U.S. way of life? It's not Nazism. Its socialism, its communism, its Marxism, all variants of the same disease. To the extent we embrace any of these false ideologies, we will suffer." [21] And Mark J. Perry puts it like this, "It is the initial illusion of success that gives socialism it's pernicious, seductive appeal. But in the long run, socialism has an unbroken track record of being a formula for tyranny, poverty, and misery."[22]

---

[21] Investors Business Daily, https://www.investors.com/politics/editorials/millennials-socialism/
[22] Mark J. Perry, FEE (Foundations of Economics Education), https://fee.org/articles/why-socialism-failed/

In a Socialist world, the first generation still has the last fruits of capitalism lingering temporally. Quickly the government begins to take over and ruin the economy though. The government is able to do this because it has no higher power over it (it has its own checks and balances through the different branches but they can only limit one another from a peer to peer standpoint, none of them is the authority over the other). It therefore can justify anything.

Just take a glance at history, the entity that has done the most damage to the largest group of people were governments overpowered by the seized power they took from the people. After taking the power from the people they attack those same people who gave up their power (willingly or unwillingly). Prime examples are German Nazism, Mao Zedong's dynasty, Joseph Stalin's USSR. This book is a pleading to young people like myself to learn from history. I don't want to be a couple of decades down the road and we are raising kids and asking, how did we let this happen? Why didn't anyone tell us? We should have already known from school, but we are ignorant of what leads to men like this. The people were desperate and gave themselves over to the will of these men and they used it to abuse them. We can let any one person or group of people have the ability to do that to us. Liberty keeps the government in a box. They are like a goldfish in a small container. They cannot grow any bigger because they would succeed in the space. If we put the government in the ocean, the government will group to be a big whale that we can no longer control.

Chapter 16: Socialism and the Fall

The young are being talked into giving up their freedom just like the Adam and Eve story. The snake wanted them to question their freedom under God to do whatever they wanted, except for eating of that tree. In eating that tree they believed they would get more freedom but instead, they were enslaved to the most tyrannical being in the universal spiritually, the Devil.

In the case of America, the snake is the socialist government politicians trying to convince people to give up their freedoms because supposedly being enslaved to the government's will is better than having one's own freedom. Supposedly it's better to have everything government-controlled because supposedly the government can build the economy better than the businesses themselves.

In the Garden of Eden, it was a free market. God basically told them just to go and be fruitful and multiply and subdue the earth. There was no government over them and there was no authority over them, they were just free to grow and thrive. They didn't need a government.

In part two we will discuss how the privatized government is better than the public ran the government. America's founding was referred to in its origination as "the social experiment." The significance of this is that the framers of the constitution and the founding fathers created a mathematical formula that was unprecedented in world history. It was a system of checks and balances comprised of 2/3rd's majorities. Three branches of government (Executive, legislative, and Judicial). No single branch could overrule another. The same is true of house seats for congress, there were two congress seats per state, and then additional seats for those appointed by state population (535 in total). The significance of multiple political parties only further iterates what the founders were hoping to accomplish. You could say that having Democratic, Republican, Libertarian, and Independent parties, creates the accountability that America was always supposed to have.

Websites

Tom Woods- one of most well-known modern-day Libertarians

Ludwig Von Mises Institute

Foundations of Economics Education

Anti-War

Curriculum

Liberty Classroom (Liberty from POV of Libertarianism)

<u>Ron Paul's self-taught home schooling curriculum</u>

Podcasts

The Tom Woods Show

The Libertarian Christian Podcast

The Anarcho Christian Podcast

The Bob Murphy Show

Radio Rothbard

Ron Paul Liberty Podcast

Part 2:

Privatized over Publicized

Chapter 17: Privatization in General

"Privatization would allow entrepreneurs to take on challenges at which federal bureaucracies are failing. The United States is a land of huge talent and diversity. But to take full advantage of those assets, we should divest the government of activities that individuals and businesses can perform better by themselves." [23]

---

[23] Chris Edwards, Cato Institute,

Just so we can be clear about the word

Privatization let's look at Chris Edward's

definition,

> "This study mainly uses privatization in a
> narrow sense to mean fully moving
> ownership of businesses and assets to the
> private sector. The term is often used
> more broadly to include government
> contracting, public-private partnerships,
> vouchers, and other forms of partial
> privatization. Those are all worthy
> reforms, but they are not the focus here."

Cato.org[24]

https://www.cato.org/sites/cato.org/files/pubs/pdf/pa794_1.pdf

Jon B. Goodman from Harvard business review starts us off at the heart of the matter when he says,

> "In the functions that are privatized, they (the government) argue, the profit-seeking behavior of new, private sector madras one daily leads to cost-cutting and greater attention to customer satisfaction." [25]

As stated in the last section, completion over the customer's dollar drives better service

---

[24] Chris Edwards, Cato Institute, https://www.cato.org/sites/cato.org/files/pubs/pdf/pa794_1.pdf

[25] John B. Goodman, Harvard Business Review, https://hbr.org/1991/11/does-privatization-serve-the-public-interest

and better products. On the other hand, with the

government, they're not going to shut down no

matter how bad their service or product is

because they are propped up by the federal

government. As this section unfolds you will

see how the private sector beats out the public.

What is truly best for the economy is having the

businesses that have the best quality product

and customer service alongside the best rates so

that the dollar on a national level will go the

farthest. The government is always pitching

that we need to create more jobs, but you do not

hear them talk about raising the quality of the

jobs that are already in the economy.

If you are skeptical that privatization of the public work then check out this quote by John B. Goodman, from Harvard Business Review, on the privatization that has already taken place around the world.

"This newfound faith privatization has spread to become the global economic phenomenon of the 1990s. Throughout the world, governments are training over to private managers to control everything from electrical utilities to prisons, from railroads to education. By the end of the 1980s, sales of state enterprises worldwide had reached out a total of over $185 billion – with no signs of a slowdown. In 1990 alone the worlds' governments sold off $25 billion in state-owned enterprises – with continents vying to see who could claim the privatization title."[26]

More governments outside of America, are seeing the power of the free market. They see that if there is a private company already doing what their public company is doing, why they don't leave them to it. The government already has so much of the responsibility why is it trying to have departments and companies compete with the private sector? If there is

---

[26] John B. Goodman, Harvard Business Review, https://hbr.org/1991/11/does-privatization-serve-the-public-interest

already a company doing the job well or better
in the public sector then what's the point of
competing with him? The government is meant
to fill in the gaps where the people have a need.

Different countries around the world like
Britain, Australia, Canada, Mexico, and Eastern
Europe have privatized, Chris Edwards (Cato
Institute) describes what's been done.

"She (Margaret Thatcher) was
determined to revive the stagnant British
economy, and her government privatized
dozens of major businesses, including
British Airways, British Telecom, British
Steel, and British Gas. Other nations
followed the British lead. . . . Australia

privatized dozens of companies between the mid-1990s and mid-2000s, generating proceeds of more than $100 billion. . . During the 1980s and 1990s, Canada privatized more than 50 major businesses, including electric utilities, a railway, an airline, and the air traffic control system. . . Mexico, for example, slashed the number of state-owned firms from 1,155 in the early 1980s to just 210 by the early 2000s. . . In Eastern Europe, huge privatizations were pursued after the fall of communism, and the government share of total economic output in that region fell from about three-quarters in 1990 to about one-

quarter today."[27]

People say that Europe and socialism go hand and hand but Margaret Thatcher was trying to undo socialism.

"Thatcher had a strong personal belief in privatization. Privatization was crucial for 'reversing the corrosive and corrupting effects of socialism,' she said, and central to 'reclaiming territory for freedom. The purpose of privatization was to ensure 'the state's power is

---

[27] Chris Edwards,
https://www.cato.org/sites/cato.org/files/pubs/pdf/pa794_1.pdf

reduced and the power of the people enhanced.'" [28]

As we can see Socialism is the opposite of privatization. Thatcher was in a society that was socialistic and she perceived it as corrosive and corrupted. She looked around in her own country and saw how the current government was given too much power, leading them to the temptation to become corrupted by the power and the ability to monopolize everything, which led to a very negative effect on the economy.

---

[28] Same Source

Chapter 18: Toll Road Highway versus Taxpayer Highway

"Roads start wearing out practically from the day they open to traffic. Regular preventive maintenance keeps pavement from deteriorating prematurely. When that maintenance is skimped on, instead of lasting 50 years before needing complete reconstruction, a road may need to be rebuilt in 20 or 25 years. State highway agencies do the best they can, but their budgets come from state legislators. And those elected officials would much rather authorize spending for new roads and bridges on which they can hold a ribbon-cutting ceremony than authorize enough money year-in and year-out for proper preventative and maintenance on existing roads. So 'tax roads' end up wearing out prematurely and having to be rebuilt at great cost to taxpayers.'" [29]

---

[29] Robert Poole https://reason.org/commentary/are-toll-roads-most-expensive-roads/

I am not going to lie as a citizen of a tollway heavy area, the toll charges add up quickly. But they are by far the best quality roads I have ever been on. Highways are so vital in big metropolises like Dallas and Atlanta where everything is spread out. It makes sense that if you use a road more than other people then the amount that you pay into that road's maintenance should be more. If you barely use a highway, you should not be charged. Tolls allow for a "per use cost", in other words a 1:1 ratio of cost to use. The people who use it more pay more. That makes more sense than everyone, irrespective of how much they use the highway, have to pay towards it with equal percentages, based on individual's tax bracket.

Roads are made of cement and pavement. Those materials are worn down every single time a car goes over them so it is not like there's an option where we don't pay money to maintain the roads. The question is not which option cost money, but instead which one is the best use of the money spent.

The beginning quote of this chapter shows us that the toll roads last twice as long as the state roads. If you can buy one thing and it lasts twice as long, why would you take part in the thing that has half a shelf life? Especially considering that highways normally funnel much more traffic than normal roads. They are designed to keep people moving without the

crossroads of four-way stoplights or stop signs.
Government roads will wait for as long as
possible to fix things. They will let holes tear
up tons of cars until there are enough
complaints to warrant them fixing the road
because they are under budget. Versus the
tollways partaking in constant maintenance
because they are adequately funded by real time
charges to the cars actually using the service.

Robert Poole from reason.org describes the
difference like this,

> "By contrast, toll roads are legally
> protected from inadequate maintenance.
> Those who buy toll road bonds insist on
> the first priority for using all total

revenues is proper maintenance. Why?
Because they realize that the total
revenues they are counting on to pay the
debt service and the bonds depend on the
toll road offering high-quality service
that makes people willing to pay tolls to
use that road rather than non— tolled
alternatives. So the 'Bond covenants'-
legally enforceable agreement between
the toll road owner and the bondholders –
guarantee proper maintenance. And that
means the toll road will last its full
design life in good shape at a lower life-
cycle cost than the tax road that has to be
reconstructed prematurely. It's as if the
toll road comes equipped with an

endowment fund to pay for its maintenance. Unfortunately, there is nothing comparable to tax codes."

Basically, their accountability is legally obligatory. There is no procrastination until they are hated by the people who use the road because the road is so terrible that people's cars are being torn up. If the tollway companies did not upkeep their part they could sue them for the money lost. There is no minimum obligation for the public-owned roads on the other hand. In case you're unconvinced that this is a legitimate needed option, let's hear from the businessman-politician himself, Trump.

"President Trump's latest infrastructure plan outlines ways in which private-public partnership can help fix America's crumbling roads and bridges, including the liberalization of tolling policy so that private investment can have an active role in rebuilding America." [30]

Trump is a businessman so he knows that we should not spend money unless we need to. In other parts of the economy Trump wants to fix the already public businesses, so if he wants to use the private arm to assist the public then he really thinks it's a good option.

---

[30] Savannah Barker, https://thetylt.com/politics/toll-roads-infrastructure-good-bad

In case Trump is not someone you think you can trust from a financial standpoint check out this quote,

"Transportation economists have often argued that toll roads are in fact the answer to improving America's roads." [31]

So the people who think about the cost efficiency of moving from place to place have even advocated for it. There is not going to be anyone who is more knowledgeable about the subject than these guys. Congress has even tried to implement a bill that factors in the extra cost of roads that ought to be factored in but is not.

---

[31] Savannah Barker, https://thetylt.com/politics/toll-roads-infrastructure-good-bad

"Over a decade ago, Congress enlisted the help of a bipartisan commission of experts to find a solution to the transportation funding problem, and they came up with a 'Vehicle Miles Traveled tax' that would charge drivers per mile traveled. It seems perfectly reasonable that those Americans to use the roads regularly help to pay to maintain them." [32]

So instead of having to do the charge in a roundabout way, why not just let it happen as it happens on the road from day to day. The upkeep of miles traveled and wear on the road is calculated through the tolls every time it's

[32] Savannah Barker, https://thetylt.com/politics/toll-roads-infrastructure-good-bad

used. The private companies are keeping track of the miles traveled so why would we need to pass a separate law to keep up with the miles?

In order to help our minds accept this idea of paying for the roads we just need to recategorize it.

> "Americans pay for the amount of water and electricity use, why shouldn't we subsidize the amount of road we use?"[33]

If we need to put money into our cars and technology to keep them at optimum functionality then why should we not pay for

---

[33] Savannah Barker, https://thetylt.com/politics/toll-roads-infrastructure-good-bad

our roads? Roads are the most important thing needed to have a good economy. Imagine if the world did not have roads that were made of asphalt or cement. We would go to drive and we would get stuck if there was any sort of liquid. It would be so hard to go at any great speed without risking damage to our car. It would be a nightmare. We have to imagine a world without something in order to appreciate it.

I say all this to say that society has needs. The government historically has helped the public meet those needs with public departments that have staff who do the numbers and hire the people to maintain these needs.

The problem becomes when the government is stuck in the tradition that doesn't want to acknowledge that the need for public services is oftentimes being met and competing with businesses in the free market that are doing their job better. If the government would acknowledge that the toll companies and many other companies are already taking from the public services then they can liquidate those departments and let the fully functioning free market take over the responsibility. In the short term, jobs will be lost, but the private companies will have a need to hire people to do those same services that the public companies had been doing. It's really just taking the burden off the government funnel and allowing it to focus on the stuff that the private market is not able to help with. Which is mainly going to be within the parameter of the two principles, as discussed in section one, protection of the citizen's property and body. In the next chapter of this section, I will continue to prove to you other areas that the free market and private business are better than the public government-run services.

Chapter 19: Public Delivery Service versus Private Delivery Service

"The Post office didn't really do anything wrong. The market shifted. The Post Office value proposition simply isn't as valuable as it once was we don't really care if mail delivery comes daily. In fact, many of us forget to check our mailbox for several consecutive days. We don't much care that a physical letter can transit the continent overnight."[34]

---

[34] Adam Hartung, https://www.forbes.com/sites/adamhartung/2011/12/06/why-the-postal-service-is-going-out-of-business/#712660144317

The Postal Service was great before the technological boom. Now it is fraught with tradition and unionization. Just the other day I was talking to a guy who used to be in management at the Postal Service. He said that he was able to prove all kinds of falsified records from an employee he was monitoring because he was suspicious. He showed his clear evidence to his superior, the superior told him to fire him. He did "fire" him, but the guy went to the union and didn't even miss one workday. That is what led him to quit and move to the private sector. That was the needle that broke the camel's back. For him, if he could not fire them, then he had no leverage to manage them.

In case this case study does not do the trick for you, check out the big-picture look at the Postal Service,

'The USPS is on an unsustainable financial path and must be restructured to prevent a taxpayer-funded bailout,' the president said in an order that was released Thursday night. The order calls for an examination of the Postal Service's pricing, policies and works force costs. The Postal Service has lost more than $65 billion over the past decade as Americans increasingly transmit messages online." [35]

____

[35] Carolyn Cerbin,
https://www.usatoday.com/story/news/politics/onpolitics/201
8/04/12/trump-forms-task-force-study-postal-service-

That is your money being wasted in 10 years' time! Imagine if that money was still in the economy, what good that would do. I think that the 'taxpayer-funded bailout' is the best way to put my whole argument when it comes to government-run economics. The government has no money of its own, it takes it from us. The government will never ask us if we thought the Postal Service should be cut off from government aid to see if it can fare alongside the private companies. It would be too embarrassing to see their responsibility crash and burn as any other free-market company would that was that unprofitable. They would just take the money they forced out of our hands and go save a lifeboat of people whose

boat has been blown to shreds. It's financially

ridiculous and irresponsible of the government

to see the failure of the Postal Service and think

it can be saved with a little tweaking.

In order to get a grasp of how out of the league

Amazon is to the Postal service check out this

quote,

> "Prime members get free shipping, often
> in as few as one or two days. Amazon is
> also expanding options for free same-day
> delivery and beefing up Prime Now,
> which delivers food and household items
> within two hours. The postal service
> cannot match the speed that they want.

For a customer to get something delivered on the same day they order it from Amazon, it needs to be in the post office system at 6 am." [36]

The Postal Service could not handle the workload of Amazon. We can see a lot about the Postal Services position in the market by the way that Amazon treats them, they pay the Postal Service less than their competition. Believe it or not, the Postal Service is kept afloat by Amazon. Look at these two quotes about Amazon and USPS relationship,

---

[36] Memphis Business Journal, https://www.bizjournals.com/memphis/news/2018/07/02/amazon-delivery-plan-poses-threat-to-us-postal.html

"David Vernon, an analyst at Bernstein Research who tracks the shipping industry, estimated in 2015 that Amazon was paying the postal service $2 per package, which is about half what it would pay publicly traded United Parcel Service Inc. and FedEx Corp. A Citigroup research note released last April estimated that every delivery by the Postal Service is parcel business – not just a products from Amazon – should cost $1.46 more to reflect its true economic costs."[37]

[37] Joshua Gallu and Mark Milian, Bloomberg, https://www.bloomberg.com/news/articles/2018-04-03/how-the-post-office-makes-amazon-a-federal-issue-quicktake

And

> "E-commerce revenue provides essential support to pay for the network and infrastructure that enables us to fulfill our (the Postal Services) universal service obligations." [38]

Amazon underpays the original delivery service. Clearly, Amazon does not value the Postal Service, and by the low quantity they pay sends a message that the delivery industry could survive without it. If Amazon thought the Postal Service was indispensable then they would pay them the same or more than FedEx or UPS. When a public company is dependent

---

[38] Same Source

on a privately owned company there should be red flags big time. So let's get to snipping.

As we saw in this section, two major case studies of industries where private systems are more efficient, longer-lasting, and make the dollar go farther. If most of the world is already privatizing their economy and most industries have a better version of the public sector competing and outperforming them than let's vote to get rid of what is unnecessary. If it can be proven there are more efficient competitors that do not save the jobs just because they are "government jobs". There should be nothing sacred or untouchable about the public sector. The government needs to get with the times and accept that people have shown up and put the public sphere in its place. Keeping the public around is a suck on the economy and waste of our money. The only way to cut them out is to as a group tell them they are unnecessary.

In the next section, I will be having an in house conversation with my fellow religious people, mainly Christians. I will be defending how one can be a Bible-believing Christian and still be a freedom fighter. I also will explain why I think Libertarianism and abortion are contrary ideas.

Part 3:

Compatibility of Conservative Christian with Libertarianism

Chapter 20: Abortion and Libertarianism

Whether you are religious or antitheist (atheist) the values of Liberty protect people of all ages, genders, and ethnicities. This includes babes inside their mother and outside their mother. I am not an expert on the biology of an infant when it is inside the womb, but we all know logically that a baby is a separate person from its mother. My son did come from my wife's DNA but that does not make him the same person as her. Her DNA was used to make a separate organism. In a similar way to a single-celled organism splitting to become another one, even though they are the exact same DNA make up(versus babies are half mom's DNA and half Dads) once cells divide they become a different organism. Once the egg and the sperm come together you have a whole new being. Also in a similar way, trees start off as a seed once the seed begins to sprout it is on its way to becoming a full-grown tree.

So just like the seed from the tree is a potential tree, the seed or egg from a woman is a potential separate human. Once the sperm hits the egg then the potential goes away and we have a never-ending upward trajectory of growth. My son, as of the writing of this section, is 10 months old. 19 months ago his actualization process of the sprout to full grown began. That process won't stop until he is about 25 or so (the human brain does not fully develop until this age). At that point, the body goes into a more degenerative phase leading to old people. This analog is actually why I have a shirt that says pretend I'm a tree and save me. It blows me away how some people can go hug a tree to keep it from being cut down but turn and murder the little sprout inside of them.

Just to show the inconsistency, if a pregnant woman is hit in a car wreck then it is a double homicide, but if she makes it to her destination, an abortion clinic, and kills her baby then she walks away with no criminal charges. It is the only place in the world where someone can kill another human being and be innocent of murder. A life was snuffed out forever and the women are praised because she had the courage to get "health care".

No one in their right mind thinks of it as health care. Do theme parks think its healthcare if a woman goes on a high-intensity ride to the detriment of the baby, no? Do airport administration think its healthcare when a woman is about to have the baby and she goes in an airplane, no? Why can a woman go to prison for killing her 3 months through shaky baby syndrome but women can kill her baby a

week before he is born with no charges?

I say all this because, at the end of the

day, I believe in freedom. Clearly, the first

section of the book shows how much I value

freedom. The problem is freedom has its limits.

Freedom is meant to not to violate others rights

by exterior forces. Abortion goes against that

kind of freedom. Abortion has a baby not only

being harmed but murdered by external forces.

The external force being the mother's will and

the hand of the abortionist. This is what sets

libertarianism apart from chaos. Libertarianism

allows for people's rights to be protected by

protecting their belongings both body and

property. If your things are being stolen with no consequence or you're being beaten up without consequence, it will be very difficult to exercise your freedoms. You will be in constant fear of losing property or being harmed.

I think the hard part about libertarianism is that you have an atheist evolutionist who thinks that we all are evolved stardust that have no objective moral significance and then you have Christians who think that we were made like God (in His Image, Genesis 1:27) and are created thus to think and act like him. Since libertarianism does not take a theological stance on God then when it tries to make arguments morally for the two principles it struggles. It does assume that every human in society innately ought to think that theft and bodily harm is inherently wrong. The problem is that those people who claim to be libertarian's but have killed or advocate killing babies in the womb are poking a hole in that assumption.

As a Christian, I would say they are suppressing the truth in unrighteousness. But that's the struggle libertarianism is built on moral assumptions that not everyone has. What is hard is that people want to have the freedom of libertarianism and they want the protections of libertarianism, but they do not want to give up freedoms. Someone wants the freedom to harm someone against their will aka the freedom to kill unborn humans. They assume that the value of that human being inside a woman is only valuable if it's temporal life support and the partial creator wants them or not. So, to willing parents, 'we are so glad your baby is in the world, kids are great.' Then we turn around and say to our unwilling parent friend who just killed her kid, yeah I guess that one was not worthy enough to make it into the world. The second moral stance is a philosophical word called existentialism, which is defined as there being no objective morality, instead the standard for value and truth is what individuals say the meaning is. So in this example the mother did not existentialistically decide this life had value for herself, so we all accept her subjective value as the new standard.

In this system meaning does not come from an

innate universal truth but instead is made up

from person to person.

Thus this is a tension within

Libertarianism. People want to protect wanted

life, but exterminate life they do not want. This

is the struggle between objective truth

Libertarianism and subjective relativist

Libertarianism.

Chapter 21: Freedom and Religion

As stated in the historical significance chapter, America was founded by people who wanted freedom from a state-established religion, the Church of England. For the first century, the country struggled with having this freedom of religion towards others. People might be even fined for not attending church. They came to America to be free to do religion their own way, but ironically switched their mindset to trying to enforce a religious norm on everyone through laws.

On the other hand, freedom did blossom from that society. It was in the desire to escape from the extreme rules of the Puritanical Separatist. Luckily, the true freedom of America, that was in principle made in line with the reason the Separatists left England in the first place, came when states like Pennsylvania started being free states of refuge where people could flee persecution and live out their different beliefs without discrimination or fine.

Without freedom of religion, we will lose all control of ourselves. When Christianity was first founded, the Mediterranean area was under Roman dominion. If the people were willing to pay homage to Caesar than they could do whatever they wanted. The problem is that any religion that has a deity will not allow for that. The Christians were not allowed to pinch the incense to Caesar and still say they were faithful to God. Unfortunately it led to them being hated by Caesar. Caesar needed absolute loyalty and submission due to the size of his empire. In his mind, if left as is, rebellion could lead to revolt and revolt to loss of territory. Fortunately, America is in advanced times. People could revolt or protest and it wouldn't be at risk of states leaving the country.

Chapter 23: Scripture and Libertarianism

Brian Hawkins the Christian case for libertarianism

"Libertarianism is the natural political ideology for Christians because it promotes individual freedom. 1 Peter 2:16 reads, 'As freemen, yet not using liberty as a cloak for vice, but as bondservants of God.' Men free from the chains of government can maximize our liberties to help our fellow man through private charity and evangelism."[39]

Throughout this section, I will exclusively be using the NASB, aka the New American Standard Bible.

If there is one theme I have put throughout this book it is the one proven by the quote above, people free from hindrance can flourish in all manner of life. Especially in accords of religion. In the case of religion, the government has the biggest bone to pick,

---

[39] Brian Hawkins, The Federalist, https://thefederalist.com/2015/12/16/the-christian-case-for-libertarianism/

unfortunately, the worst thing the government can do is regulate the main driving factor of most of the world, religion.

In case you're not convinced of the compatibility of Christianity and Libertarianism this chapter is going to walk you through a Bible study to show that they are compatible. Just to clarify, I am not putting this as the last chapter as the one about the Word of God because it is the least important argument but just the opposite, it is the most important. In my mind, people remember the messages at the end of any written or oral message best. For me, if people are going to remember any argument from this section, let alone this book it would be this one. As a Christian, the governing authority for my whole life is the Bible so it would be hypocritical and inconsistent of me to choose any other path that undermines my ultimate standard and value. This is my number one reason for writing this book is that I want myself and future generations to be free to live out our convictions no matter how religious or nonreligious.

Our Hope and the Resurrection

1 Corinthians 15:16-19,32

> 16 "For if the dead are not raised, not even Christ has been raised; 17 and if Christ has not been raised, your faith is

worthless; you are still in your sins. 18 Then those also who have fallen asleep in Christ have perished. 19 If we have hoped in Christ in this life only, we are of all men most to be pitied. 32 If from human motives I fought with wild beasts at Ephesus, what does it profit me? If the dead are not raised, LET US EAT AND DRINK, FOR TOMORROW WE DIE."

Earlier in the book, I mentioned that I was an atheist until I was 16. The core idea that led me to become a follower of Jesus was this idea, the resurrection. This text's logic compelled me to want to follow Christ. Belief in Christianity does really rise or fall with this one act of Christ. Paul has a serious moment where he takes a step back from all his polishing for the last 14 chapters and ends his letter (like I'm ending this book with the most profound truths) to Corinth with this astounding compelling truth. He honestly admits that if Jesus was still in the tomb that he would walk away from all religion and just go live it up in crazy debauchery because we are all dead in our sins. And being dead in our sins means we will be punished for eternity for our sins, aka this life is our last hoorah before the warrant for our arrest catches up with us and we are put away forever.

I think this Scripture aligns with Libertarianism because Paul admits that if you do not want eternal life through the resurrection then you might as well live it up in this life. To him there are two options, you are raised to eternal life like Christ or you are punished for your sins for eternity. So as Christians we can make the same offer, you submit to your creator's provision for sin, the sacrifice for Christ or you face His wrath for those sins.

Scriptures like this give me confidence to offer the gospel of Jesus Christ to non-believers that Jesus has made a sacrifice for a whole lifetime of sin on the cross, while at the same time if they do not accept it I have peace of mind that their incorrect anti God and anti-bible beliefs will ultimately catch up with them on judgment day. I do not need to go pass a law in the government that will regulate their morality like I'm their parent. I do not want the government to pass laws to tell me what to believe so why would I want to pass laws that tell them what to believe.

To me, this text helps to unwind and untangle the ultra-conservatives who think they need to have their views represented in the government. It's okay, God is the only real government and He does not need your help trying to police people's outward behaviors, He has got it under control.

Our job is to offer the amazing gift of Christ and then back away. Now if they accept Jesus and thus want to live like an adopted child of God, well that's a different story. Now they are a part of the church. Now they are Disciples of Christ and thus we have a responsibility to hold them accountable to their new life in God. In the next part, I am going to discuss a text that deals with the Biblical double standard that God calls us to have.

Christianity and its Enclosed Community

11 "But actually, I wrote to you not to associate with any so-called brother if he is an immoral person, or covetous, or an idolater, or a reviler, or a drunkard, or a swindler--not even to eat with such a one. 12 For what have I to do with judging outsiders? Do you not judge those who are within the church? 13 But those who are outside, God judges. REMOVE THE WICKED MAN FROM AMONG YOURSELVES."

When I was a freshman in high school, and still an atheist, I was dating a girl. The topic of beliefs came up, I asked her what she believed and she responded that she was a Buddhist. My knee jerk response was to revert back to my church kid days when I was in basically the equivalent of Bible Boy Scout's, Awanas. I said that I was a Christian. Funny enough if you would have looked at any of my beliefs or worldview there would have been no trace of a Biblical worldview. I didn't even know the difference between the Old Testament and the New Testament. I was not a Christian even though I said I was, I was an atheist, I just had a relapse of belief. Once the topic of religion came up I gravitated towards the only one that I had ever been exposed to.

I say all that to say that Christianity is not a club that you can just get into by just saying you are one. It is a very enclosed exclusive group with very particular beliefs and worldview. Sure different denominations within Protestantism have disagreements but the true church agrees on the core doctrines. That's why Paul can say what he says above to the Corinthian church. Christians should not be people who openly live in sin. Yes we backslide into old sin habits at times, and when we are new believers we have many sins to be mortified (fancy word for amputated or cut off), but Christians should not be openly condoning and living in sin. They should feel guilty from the Holy Spirit in their hearts and recant (reject) those beliefs, leading to repentance or a turning away from those actions.

Those who claim to be Christians we have a duty as fellow heirs and spiritual siblings under God to help one another along in being like God. God is without evil or sin, so when we become part of His family we are expected to act like it. To me, the analogue of this is joining the mobsters. When you become part of the mob you are all into their lifestyle. Every day you are growing more in their ranks and thinking like them. Which leads you to act differently. In a similar way joining Christianity is this total commitment to be part of a belief system and a community that idolizes the God of the Bible.

The contrast is that those who are not in the church are not held to this standard. As Paul says, God is their judge. We are just children in the king's kingdom. God will never die so we will never take His place as ruler of all humanity, so stop acting like it. He is on the throne and He rules the universe. We love and submit to Him.

Those outside the church are the rebellion. They live on the outskirts of God's kingdom, always running from Him, but to no avail. The reason people do not realize they are within God's kingdom is that as Romans 1 says, they are suppressing the truth. They have been ever since the fall in the Garden of Eden, with Adam and Eve, when they ate from the forbidden tree and lost their freedom under God and became enslaved to the Devil. Christians have been illuminated to the devil's deceitfulness and freed from his spiritual haze. In the next part, we will deal with why non-Christians cannot believe in God.

Exclusive Beliefs of the Church

Romans 6:5-7

5 "For if we have become united with Him in the likeness of His death, certainly we shall also be in the likeness of His resurrection, 6 knowing this, that our old self was crucified with Him, in order that our body of sin might be done away with, so that we would no longer be slaves to sin; 7 for he who has died is freed from sin."

As stated in the section above, Christians once were enslaved to sin, but now we have been freed from sin because our old self has died with Christ. This is the analogy of Baptism. When someone is dunked under the water, the dunking is representing our old wicked self being put to death (like how people are put under the grave, the water represents the ground) and when we emerge from the water that represents being raised to new life in Christ. The problem is that people who have not experienced regeneration (receiving the Holy Spirit after believing the gospel of Jesus unto conversion) are still in their "enslaved" state. So all people who are of different religious and moral backgrounds that you meet in person and online are still enslaved to the devil spiritually. They are no different than Adam after the fall, when he became enslaved to the Devil back in the Garden spiritually. The realization that salvation in our hearts is the only way to have a God-fearing heart is why we can be gracious to those of different views. People with different views are shackled to the devil's will and beliefs.

Paul describes the transformation that God does when he frees us from enslavement to freedom in Christ in Ephesians 2.

Ephesians 2:1-6

1 "And you were dead in your trespasses and sins, 2 in which you formerly walked according to the course of this world, according to the prince of the power of the air, of the spirit that is now working in the sons of disobedience. 3 Among them we too all formerly lived in the lusts of our flesh, indulging the desires of the flesh and of the

mind, and were by nature children of wrath, even as the rest. 4 But God, being rich in mercy, because of His great love with which He loved us, 5 even when we were dead in our transgressions, made us alive together with Christ (by grace you have been saved), 6 and raised us up with Him, and seated us with Him in the heavenly places in Christ Jesus."

We were dead, spiritual zombies. We were following the way of this world, which is fed by the devil, that trajectory of deserving wrath, because it was displeasing to God. But God graciously and lovingly made us alive again. God is the only hope for nonbelievers to believe. Without God giving us this transformation it is like having a blow horn in the ear of a zombie and telling them not to eat flesh. It will not work, they are by nature flesh eaters. They are enslaved to lust after the flesh. In the same way, nonbelievers are enslaved to lust after sinful and rebellious things against God. Because the devil has them enslaved to love these things. In the same way, passing laws is not going to transform the heart of non-believers. People will sin, (and/or break the law) and hide it from the government. All the law does is make it more difficult and breeds bitterness and distrust of the government.

Without God, I would still be an atheist. I had no hope of breaking my mold of being a spiritual zombie. But God sent in Himself in the form of the Holy Spirit to show me properly who Jesus was. Paul describes this illumination of the Spirit in 2 Corinthians 4.

2 Corinthians 4:3-7

3 "And even if our gospel is veiled, it is veiled to those who are perishing, 4 in whose case the god of this world has blinded the minds of the unbelieving so that they might not see the light of the gospel of the glory of Christ, who is the image of God. 5 For we do not preach ourselves but Christ Jesus as Lord, and ourselves as your bond-servants for Jesus' sake. 6 For God, who said, "Light

shall shine out of darkness," is the One who has shone in our hearts to give the Light of the knowledge of the glory of God in the face of Christ. 7 But we have this treasure in earthen vessels so that the surpassing greatness of the power will be of God and not from ourselves."

As we can see, God is the only hope we have for changing anyone's heart. Without God, all our speech is just muffled and veiled by the one voice they have been led by their whole life, the Devil. I am not saying that people are hearing voices and that's the devil, I am saying that the devil taught their spirit and mind to think like them without them even being aware of it. He persuaded people to believe in certain lies over and over again over the years until they believed they were right and true, or at least what was best for them and their scenario.

Text like these allow me to stop putting my hope in the government and instead invest my time in sharing with my fellow citizens the truths of the universe that come from the heart of God, this method is more effective than law passing. Our hope is not this world's government but instead the governor of the universe, God. Most importantly for us, in violating the freedoms of spiritual zombies, we are risking that our values will be violated and ultimately criminalized. Please apply the golden rule when it comes to the government. Do not

violate someone else's freedom to live out their

beliefs, if you yourself do not want to lose your

freedoms when the tides are turned

Conclusion

This book was meant to be a quick run

through for beginners, of the arguments and

logic of Libertarianism generally. As we can

see from the arguments in this book,

libertarianism protects the freedoms of

individuals functionally, economically, and

morally. Libertarianism is a truly inclusive and tolerant political theory. It does not favor the left side only "toleration" but instead says that freedom for all is more valuable than freedom for some, because to be able to wake up every day knowing that we are not going to be criminalized by the very authority that we trust to protect our body and property, is the most valuable and reassuring thing that we can experience as sojourners through this world. Thanks for learning about liberty with me.

More to come. . .

Bibliography

Tom Palmer, Why Liberty: Your Life, Your Choices, Your Future

Kevin D. Gomez

(http://www.genfkd.org/explaining-difference-between-libertarians-and-republicans)

Investors Business Daily, https://www.investors.com/politics/editorials/millennials-socialism/

Mark J. Perry, FEE (Foundations of Economics Education), https://fee.org/articles/why-socialism-failed/

John B. Goodman, Harvard Business Review, https://hbr.org/1991/11/does-privatization-serve-the-public-interest

Chris Edwards, Cato Institute, https://www.cato.org/sites/cato.org/files/pubs/pdf/pa794_1.pdf

Memphis Business Journal,
https://www.bizjournals.com/memphis/new
s/2018/07/02/amazon-delivery-plan-poses-
threat-to-us-postal.html

Joshua Gallu and Mark Milian, Bloomberg,
https://www.bloomberg.com/news/articles/2
018-04-03/how-the-post-office-makes-
amazon-a-federal-issue-quicktake

Brian Hawkins, The Federalist,
https://thefederalist.com/2015/12/16/the-
christian-case-for-libertarianism/

Final reminder of those links. And also

the Mises link and Foundations for Economic

Education have an insane amount of free books

in different ebook formats. (Just a little tip, if

you're mainly a kindle ebook reader like

myself, mobi is the kind of file it uses.

Sometimes the books won't have mobi files.

You have two options. You can use a free file

converter to convert the pdf to mobi or the

easier option, that I found out towards the end

of converting a bunch of books, open the pdf

file in a kindle app, right click on the download

and it will say 'open with', click the kindle app

on your phone. It will give you an option to

convert to mobi on the spot. The first option is

still good though because you can convert to

any book reader format.

Websites

Tom Woods- one of most well-known modern-day Libertarians

Ludwig Von Mises Institute

Foundations of Economics Education

Anti-War

Curriculum

Liberty Classroom (Liberty from POV of Libertarianism)

Ron Paul's self-taught home schooling curriculum

Podcasts

The Tom Woods Show

The Libertarian Christian Podcast

The Anarcho Christian Podcast

The Bob Murphy Show

Radio Rothbard

Ron Paul Liberty Podcast

There are so many more, but

this is a good sampling of the

material that is provided. There is

more exhaustive of a list of Austrian economics podcasts on the Mises institute website listed below.

If you have any questions or want to hear from me when I drop a new book on these ideas, feel free to email me at

libertyreformedbaptist@gmail.com

You can also sign up to hear from me when a new book on liberty comes out by clicking here.

If you have print go to this link,

https://mailchi.mp/d8e7edad8eb

d/timslibertybooks